Created, published, and distributed by Knock Knock
6080 Center Drive
Los Angeles, CA 90045
knockknockstuff.com
Knock Knock is a registered trademark of Knock Knock LLC

Design by Carol Kono-Noble

ISBN: 978-1683491460
UPC: 825703-50244-2

10 9 8 7 6 5 4 3 2 1

Scratch.
SNIFF.
Write.

A UNIQUELY SENSORY JOURNAL

KNOCK KNOCK®
LOS ANGELES, CALIFORNIA

INTRODUCTION

This journal is a celebration of your nose, and all the gifts it gives you every day: fun, feelings, stories, memories, and wisdom.

Your nose is a time machine. More than any other sense, smell is directly tied to memory. One whiff of a long-forgotten perfume, and you may be instantly thrust into a recollection so vibrant and full as to be almost three-dimensional. And it's likely to be emotional, too. That's because smells are first processed by the olfactory bulb, which starts inside the nose and connects to two brain areas strongly implicated in emotion and memory: the amygdala and hippocampus. You never know what might trigger these feeling-memories—the smell of pencils, a new pair of sneakers, a certain dish, bubble gum.

But scent is also a matchmaker. As *Scientific American* reported, "Smell, it seems, plays an underappreciated role in romance and other human affairs." There's a scientific reason why some people just smell good to us. It sounds like magic, but researchers have proven that each person's unique scent, known as an odorprint, is like an invisible Cupid's arrow, helping us to pair up with genetically compatible mates.

Scent is also a clock, announcing seasonal shifts: the smell of icy-cold air and fir trees in December, jasmine blossoms in May, firecracker smoke in July. These all trigger waves of emotion and memory, placing us in the cycle of time.

Given its connection to memory and emotion, it's no surprise that smell is especially rich terrain for writers. Memoirists, poets, essayists, and novelists love to muse on the scents around them, the smells that whisper, sing, or shout to them; the stories these scents contain. Helen Keller wrote with special passion about her sense of smell, which was no doubt powerfully attuned, connecting her directly to her surroundings.

The scents in this journal are meant to trigger your own private thoughts and recollections. Use them. If a given scent doesn't smell exactly like what it's called, don't worry—what does it smell like to *you*? Where does that smell take you? What does it mean—is it something from long ago, or something vital to your everyday existence now? Use this journal to celebrate your own life's rhythms, big and small. Sniff, riff, and enjoy it. Just don't taste it.

Smell is a potent wizard that transports us across a thousand miles and all the years we have lived. The odor of fruits wafts me to my Southern home, to my childhood frolics in the **PEACH** orchard. Other odors, instantaneous and fleeting, cause my heart to dilate joyously or contract with remembered grief. Even as I think of smells, my nose is full of scents that start awake sweet memories of summers gone and ripening grain fields far away.

—HELEN KELLER

I began to long, as I had before, for some special smell, some special music that would fill me, lift me up and carry me away, float me off the rocks of my body and sweep me into some wideness, some vast expanse of blue-grey nothingness.

—DENTON WELCH

GET SWEPT AWAY BY THE SMELL OF . . .

The smell of good **BREAD** baking, like the sound of lightly flowing water, is indescribable in its evocation of innocence and delight. —M. F. K. FISHER

THE SMELL OF LAUNDRY REMINDS ME OF . . .

Is there any place on Earth that smells better than a Laundromat? It's like a rainy Sunday when you don't have to get out from under your covers, or like lying back on the grass your father's just mowed—comfort food for your nose. —JODI PICOULT

I had particularly loved her smell. She always smelled **FRESH**, freshly washed or of fresh laundry or fresh sweat or freshly loved. —BERNHARD SCHLINK

The barn was very large. It was very old. It smelled of hay and it smelled of manure. It smelled of the perspiration of tired horses and the wonderful sweet breath of patient cows. It often had a sort of peaceful smell as though nothing bad could happen ever again in the world. —E. B. WHITE

> "One rule in life," he murmured to himself. "If you can smell **GARLIC**, everything is all right."
>
> —J. G. BALLARD

THESE THINGS SMELL SO DELICIOUS TOGETHER . . .

The smell of roasting meat together with that of burning fruitwood and dried herbs is as voluptuous as incense in a church. —H. D. RENNER

It smells of old houses and aged wood and dark secrets, but also of hard, hot sunshine through ancient shutters and long, wicked afternoons in a four-poster bed. It's not a **WINE**, it's a life, right there in the glass.
—NICK HARKAWAY

*In the spring, at the
end of the day, you
should smell like dirt*
—MARGARET ATWOOD

E SMELL OF DIRT MAKES ME FEEL . . .

The room filled with the smell of warming butter and sugar and **LEMON** and eggs, and at five, the timer buzzed and I pulled out the cake and placed it on the stovetop. The house was quiet. The bowl of icing was right there on the counter, ready to go, and cakes are best when just out of the oven, and I really couldn't possibly wait, so I reached to the side of the cake pan, to the least obvious part, and pulled off a small warm spongy chunk of deep gold. Iced it all over with chocolate. Popped the whole thing into my mouth.

—AIMEE BENDER

Our foyer has a funny smell that doesn't smell like anyplace else. I don't know what the hell it is. It isn't cauliflower and it isn't perfume— I don't know what the hell it is—but you always know you're home. —J. D. **SALINGER**

Perfumes are
the feelings
of **FLOWERS.**

—HEINRICH HEINE

THE MOST INTOXICATING FLOWER SCENTS ARE ...

Give me odorous at sunrise a garden of beautiful flowers where I can walk undisturb'd. —**WALT WHITMAN**

My son smelled like a **CINNAMON BUN**, and that smell entered into my biological being, and it became an imperative that I keep him alive at all costs. —FRANCES McDORMAND

Smells detonate softly in our memory like poignant land mines, hidden under the weedy mass of many years and experiences. Hit a tripwire of smell, and memories explode all at once.

—DIANE ACKERMAN

FAVORITE MEMORY SMELLS LIKE . . .

Everywhere the grain stood ripe and the hot afternoon was full of the smell of the ripe wheat, like the smell of bread baking in an oven. The breath of the wheat and the **SWEET CLOVER** passed him like pleasant things in a dream. —WILLA CATHER

THE SMELL THAT MAKES ME FEEL WORLDLY AND SMART IS . . .

The smell of opium is the least stupid smell in the world. —PABLO PICASSO

So many orchards circled the village that on some crisp October afternoons the whole world smelled like **PIE.**

—ALICE HOFFMAN

THE SCENT I DREAM IN IS . . .

It was a whiff of salt and mint, just as I approached the water on a dive, that warned that a more powerful scent would soon enter my nose. It was the scent I dreamed in. And it was the scent of that spring sky as I stood in my yard. —ANNE SPOLLEN

When I was really small I had this idea that if I could get up early enough, I could bottle the dewdrops on all the flowers and create a **PERFUME**.

—OSCAR DE LA RENTA

Or poking through a house, in closets shut for years,
Full of the smell of time—acrid, musky, dank,
One comes, perhaps, upon a flask of memories
In whose escaping scent a soul returns to life.

—CHARLES BAUDELAIRE

FLASK OF MY MEMORIES WOULD BE FILLED WITH . . .

The house
smelled musty
and damp, and
a little sweet,
as if it were
haunted by
the ghosts
of long-dead
COOKIES.

—NEIL GAIMAN

MY FAVORITE PERFUME IS . . .

What we talk about less often, because it is harder to explain, is the way a perfume can give breath and body to the phantom selves that waft about us as we go through our days—not just the showgirl, the femme fatale, and the ingenue, but all the memories and dreams of the taller, meaner, sharper, sweeter, softer people we have been or long to be.

—ALYSSA HARAD

The air—moist, sultry, secretive, and far from fresh—felt as if it were being exhaled into one's face. Sometimes it even *sounded* like heavy breathing. Honeysuckle, swamp flowers, **MAGNOLIA**, and the mystery smell of the river scented the atmosphere, amplifying the intrusion of organic sleaze. It was aphrodisiac and repressive, soft and violent at the same time. —TOM ROBBINS

*The first condition of understanding
a foreign country is to smell it.*
—T. S. ELIOT

FAVORITE TRAVEL DESTINATION SMELLS LIKE . . .

Liza poured thick batter from a pitcher onto a soapstone griddle. The **HOT CAKES** rose like little hassocks, and small volcanos formed and erupted on them until they were ready to be turned. A cheerful brown, they were, with tracings of darker brown. And the kitchen was full of the good sweet smell of them. —JOHN STEINBECK

THE SMELL OF FRESH-CUT GRASS REMINDS ME OF . . .

Freshly cut grass smells like twilight in the countryside, a football game about to start at the park, or a sunny Saturday morning in the suburbs. So . . . just stop for a second, flare your nostrils real big, tip your head back real far, and take a big whiff, baby. —NEIL PASRICHA

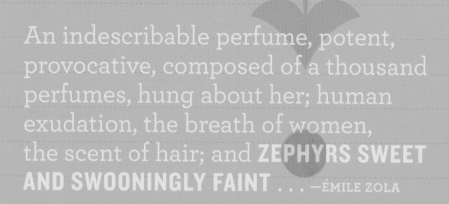

An indescribable perfume, potent, provocative, composed of a thousand perfumes, hung about her; human exudation, the breath of women, the scent of hair; and **ZEPHYRS SWEET AND SWOONINGLY FAINT** . . . —ÉMILE ZOLA

A book has got smell. A new book smells great.
An old book smells even better. An old book
smells like ancient Egypt. —RAY BRADBURY

R ME, THE SMELL OF OLD BOOKS EVOKES . . .

MY FAVORITE HOLIDAY SMELLS LIKE . . .

A smell like an eating-house and a pastrycook's next door to each other, with a laundress's next door to that! That was the pudding! —CHARLES DICKENS

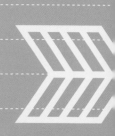